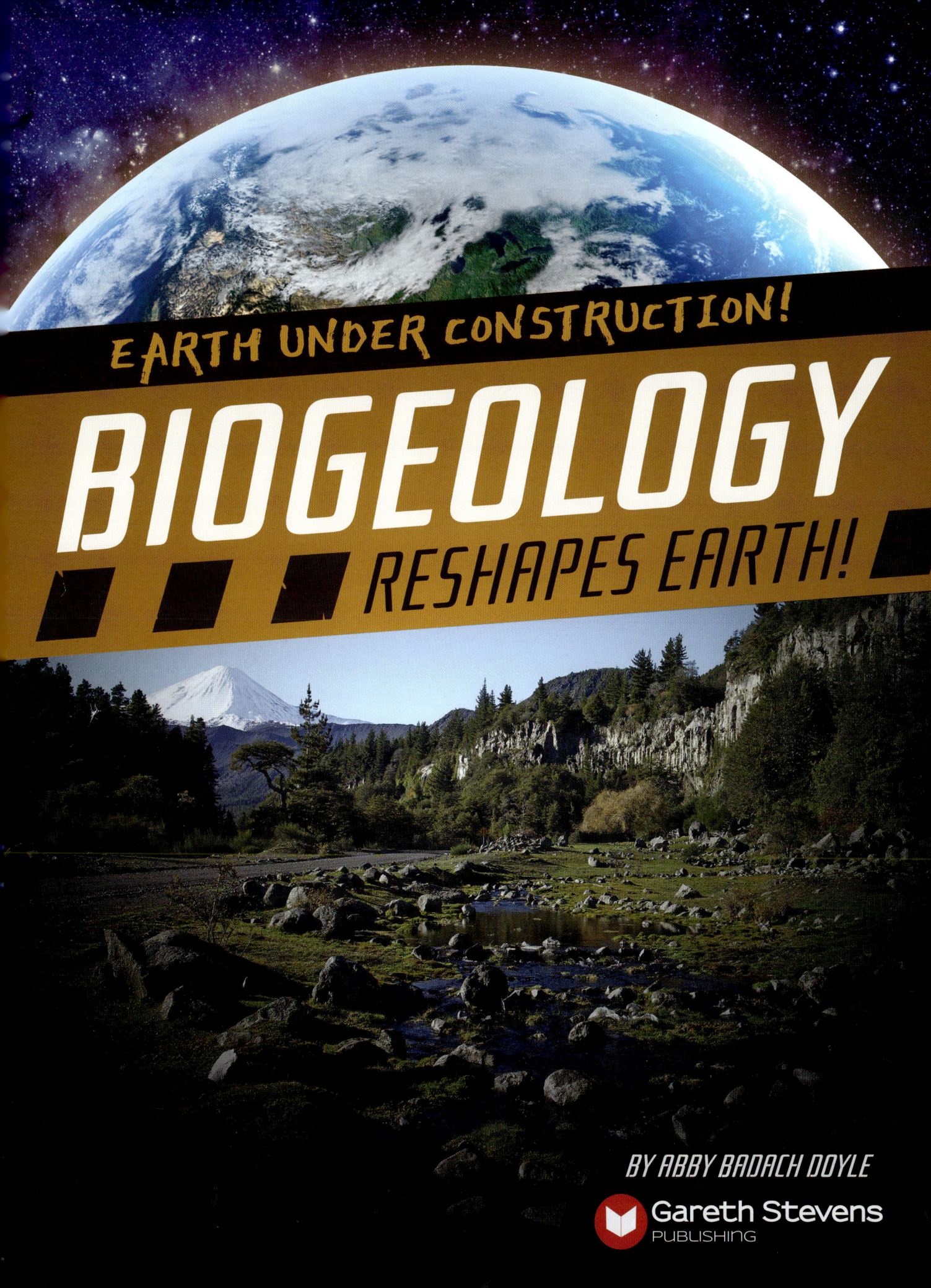

Earth Under Construction!
BIOGEOLOGY RESHAPES EARTH!

BY ABBY BADACH DOYLE

Gareth Stevens
PUBLISHING

Please visit our website, www.garethstevens.com. For a free color catalog of all our high-quality books, call toll free 1-800-542-2595 or fax 1-877-542-2596.

Library of Congress Cataloging-in-Publication Data

Names: Doyle, Abby Badach, author.
Title: Biogeology reshapes earth! / Abby Badach Doyle.
Description: New York : Gareth Stevens Publishing, [2021] | Series: Earth under construction! | Includes index.
Identifiers: LCCN 2019058968 | ISBN 9781538258200 (library binding) | ISBN 9781538258187 (paperback) | ISBN 9781538258194 (6 Pack) | ISBN 9781538258217 (ebook)
Subjects: LCSH: Environmental geology. | Biogeography.
Classification: LCC QE38 .D69 2021 | DDC 551–dc23
LC record available at https://lccn.loc.gov/2019058968

First Edition

Published in 2021 by
Gareth Stevens Publishing
111 East 14th Street, Suite 349
New York, NY 10003

Copyright © 2021 Gareth Stevens Publishing

Designer: Sarah Liddell
Editor: Kate Mikoley

Photo credits: Cover, p. 1 JeremyRichards/Shutterstock.com; space background and earth image used throughout Aphelleon/Shutterstock.com; caution tape used throughout Red sun design/Shutterstock.com; p. 5 ThomasVogel/E+/Getty Images; p. 7 (lithosphere) Clive Rees Photography/Moment/Getty Images; p. 7 (atmosphere) Jose A. Bernat Bacete/Moment/Getty Images; p. 7 (biosphere) kikkerdirk/iStock/Getty Images Plus/Getty Images; p. 7 (hydrosphere) Nora Carol Photography/Moment/Getty Images; p. 9 (top) Stan Tekiela Author/Naturalist/Wildlife Photographer/Moment/Getty Images; p. 9 (bottom) Kokhanchikov/Moment/Getty Images; p. 11 Auscape/Universal Images Group/Getty Images Plus/Getty Images; p. 13 David McNew/Staff/Getty Images News/Getty Images; p. 15 Arterra/Contributor/Universal Images Group/Getty Images; p. 17 Zoltan Tarlacz/iStock/Getty Images Plus/Getty Images; p. 19 (termite) PK289/Shutterstock.com; p. 19 (diagram) Dorling Kindersley/Getty Images; p. 19 (termite mound) Aldo Spagnol/EyeEm/Getty Images; p. 21 Troy Harrison/Moment/Getty Images; p. 23 (top) Juan Carlos Munoz/The Image Bank/Getty Images Plus/Getty Images; p. 23 (bottom) Namthip Muanthongthae/Moment/Getty Images; p. 25 Francesco Riccardo Iacomino/Moment/Getty Images; p. 27 Jeff Hunter/The Image Bank/Getty Images Plus/Getty Images; p. 29 Bloomberg/Contributor/Bloomberg/Getty Images.

All rights reserved. No part of this book may be reproduced in any form without permission in writing from the publisher, except by a reviewer.

Printed in the United States of America

Some of the images in this book illustrate individuals who are models. The depictions do not imply actual situations or events.

CPSIA compliance information: Batch #CS20GS: For further information contact Gareth Stevens, New York, New York at 1-800-542-2595.

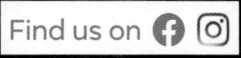

CONTENTS

What Is Biogeology? 4

One Earth, Many Spheres 6

Worm Poop Helps the Soil. 8

Plants' Roots Stop Erosion 12

Animals Dig Burrows 14

Termites Build Huge Mounds 18

Busy Beavers Create Ponds 20

Hungry Bacteria Eat Rocks. 22

Underwater Worlds .24

Humans Reshape Earth Too 28

Glossary. 30

For More Information 31

Index 32

Words in the glossary appear in **bold** type the first time they are used in the text.

WHAT IS BIOGEOLOGY?

Earth helps living things grow. You already know that! Plants need soil, water, and sunlight. Animals need a safe **habitat** to protect them from predators. But have you ever thought about how living things affect Earth? Remember, everything on our planet is connected.

Living things take from our Earth, but they also leave their mark on it. When plants grow, they can change the makeup of the soil. When beavers build dams, dry land turns into a fruitful pond. Biogeology is the study of the relationship between living things and Earth. Biogeology reshapes Earth all around us. Let's see how!

PLANTS NEED SOIL TO GROW. BUT THEY GIVE BACK TOO! PLANTS' ROOTS STOP WIND AND WATER FROM WASHING SOIL AWAY.

IT'S ALL GREEK TO ME!

The term "biogeology" comes from the Greek language. If you pick it apart, you can see how different root words come together to form a new meaning. "Bio" means life. "Geo" means Earth. And the **suffix** "-logy" means "the study of."

ONE EARTH, MANY SPHERES

To study Earth, scientists divide it into four systems. The systems are called spheres, which means area or realm. All of Earth's spheres are connected.

The atmosphere is air. The hydrosphere is water. This includes liquid like oceans, but also frozen water (ice) and water vapor (clouds). The biosphere includes all Earth's living things, from plants and animals to tiny bacteria. The lithosphere is Earth's solid land. It includes soil, rocks, and big landforms like mountains. It also includes what lies below Earth's crust. There are many ways the biosphere can reshape the lithosphere. That's biogeology!

EARTH'S SPHERES

ALL EARTH'S SPHERES AFFECT EACH OTHER. BIOGEOLOGY EXPLORES HOW LIVING THINGS RESHAPE EARTH BY WHERE THEY LIVE, HOW THEY GROW, OR WHAT THEY EAT.

MORE THAN FOUR?

Some scientists divide the spheres into even smaller parts, called sub-spheres. For example, a sub-sphere of the biosphere is the anthrosphere (AN-throw-sfeer). "Anthrop" is a Greek root word that means "human." The anthrosphere looks at people and the particular **environments** that exist only because people have built them.

WORM POOP HELPS THE SOIL

Earthworms have a strange diet. They eat dirt, dead plants, and even animal droppings. Yuck! That might sound gross, but worms are very important for healthy soil. When they eat, they take in **nutrients** from dead plant matter. Then, they put them back in the soil through their poop.

Worm poop is also called worm castings. Worm castings are some of nature's best plant food. They're rich with nutrients that help plants grow, such as potassium, calcium, and nitrates. Since these nutrients have already been through the worm's **digestive system**, it's easier for plants to use them.

WORM CASTINGS

WORM CASTINGS ARE DARK BROWN AND SHAPED LIKE TINY FOOTBALLS. UNLIKE OTHER KINDS OF ANIMAL WASTE, THEY DON'T HAVE A BAD ODOR.

WHAT'S IN YOUR DIRT?

Soil isn't made up of just one thing. It holds many tiny living microorganisms, such as bacteria and **fungi**. Like their name suggests, microorganisms are so small you need a microscope to see them. In just 0.04 ounce (1 gram) of soil, there might be up to 1 billion bacteria!

Worms dig tunnels and live underground. As they eat and poop, they move organic matter all throughout the soil. Without worms, nutrients couldn't move that much on their own. This is important for plants, which stretch their roots deep into the soil as they grow.

The worms' tunnels add open space and air to the soil. This helps keep the soil nice and loose. The tunnels and worm castings also help the soil soak up more water. That protects the soil from erosion, or wearing away from water and wind. This nutrient-rich, loose soil helps plants grow healthy and strong.

ONE WORM CAN EAT ABOUT HALF TO ONE TIME ITS BODY WEIGHT IN FOOD IN A DAY. HOW MUCH IS THAT? IMAGINE IF A 10-YEAR-OLD BOY COULD EAT AROUND 100 DOUBLE CHEESEBURGERS EVERY DAY!

WORM COMPOSTING

Good soil helps vegetables and flowers grow. That's why some gardeners keep worm farms in their backyards. You can add worms to a compost bin. Compost is a mixture of food scraps, cut grass, and leaves. The worms help break it down and turn it into healthy soil.

PLANTS' ROOTS STOP EROSION

Have you ever pulled a weed to see a clump of dirt on its roots? Roots are really good at grabbing soil. A plant's roots grow deep and wide to take in water and nutrients. One root system can grow many times bigger than the plant aboveground!

Plants reshape Earth by stopping erosion. How? Plants' roots keep soil in place. That makes it harder for rain or wind to wash it away. This is especially important for farmers who need nutrient-rich topsoil to grow food. People who live on steep slopes might plant trees or grass to help stop erosion too.

Large wildfires in 2008 and 2009 destroyed vegetation in the San Gabriel Mountains of California. Without plants' roots to hold the soil in place, heavy rains caused this mudslide in 2010.

What's So Bad About Losing Some Dirt?

Soil erosion can be harmful to people, animals, and the environment. If topsoil on farmland washes away, farmers can lose their crops and income. Loose soil can also pollute waterways with chemicals like weed killer. Heavy rain on weak soil could cause a dangerous mudslide or landslide.

ANIMALS DIG BURROWS

Many animals build underground burrows. A burrow is a system of holes and tunnels. Some live in burrows all the time. Others only use them occasionally to hide from predators or store food. The kangaroo rat weighs about 5 ounces (141.7 grams), or about as much as a baseball. However, it digs big burrows that can hold as much as 32 gallons (121 liters) of grain!

Many small **mammals** dig burrows. Some might even live in your backyard. Common animals like rabbits, gophers, groundhogs, and moles all have burrows. Moles spend almost their whole lives underground! Some birds and reptiles live in burrows too.

MOLES HAVE PADDLE-LIKE FEET AND BIG CLAWS TO HELP THEM DIG. THEY LEAVE MOUNDS OF DIRT, CALLED MOLEHILLS, AT THE SURFACE OF THEIR BURROWS.

ARE BURROWS GOOD OR BAD?

Like earthworms, burrowing animals help the soil. As they dig, they move nutrients, water, and air through the dirt. However, some people think burrowing animals are pests. Moles, rabbits, and groundhogs can destroy lawns and damage plant roots underground. They might also eat flowers or vegetables people plant in their gardens.

One famous burrowing animal is the prairie dog. Their burrows can be huge! The black-tailed prairie dog, which lives in North America's Great Plains, digs burrows about 3 to 6 feet (0.9 to 1.8 m) underground. Burrows have many tunnels about 15 feet (4.6 m) long. Like a house, a burrow has separate rooms to eat, sleep, and even use the bathroom.

Each entrance to the burrow is marked with a cone-shaped mound of dirt up to 3 feet (0.9 m) high. This keeps water out and serves as a safe spot for prairie dogs to spot danger. Together, many burrows are called prairie dog towns.

IN AREAS WHERE PRAIRIE DOGS LIVE, 1 ACRE (0.4 HA) OF LAND CAN HAVE AS MANY AS 30 TO 50 ENTRANCES TO A BURROW!

PLAYFUL PRAIRIE DOGS

Prairie dogs are very social. They play, nuzzle, and kiss! They depend on each other to share food and spot predators. The largest prairie dog town ever was in Texas. It was about 100 miles (161 km) wide and 250 miles (402 km) long. Scientists think 400 million prairie dogs lived there!

TERMITES BUILD HUGE MOUNDS

You learned how animals reshape Earth underground. But some creatures are skilled builders above ground too! Some species, or kinds, of termites construct tall mounds filled with tunnels. A termite mound can be more than 20 feet (6 m) tall. That's taller than a giraffe!

Termites live and work in colonies, like ants or bees. Using their mouths, the tiny termites move dirt and water to build the mound. They use their spit to help it stick together. However, one heavy rain can turn much of the mound to mud. Termites know to repair any harm to the mound right away.

PARTS OF A TERMITE MOUND

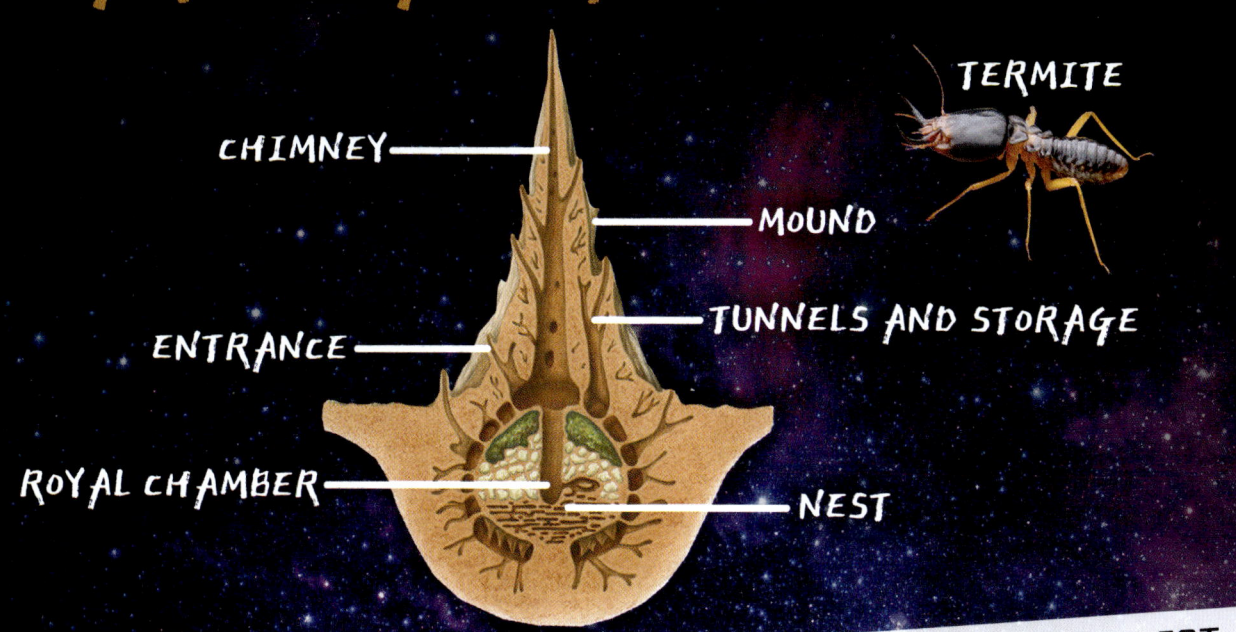

A MOUND HAS SPACE FOR THE TERMITES TO STORE FOOD AND FUNGI TO EAT. THE ROYAL CHAMBER IS WHERE THE QUEEN LIVES AND LAYS HER EGGS.

WHY DO THEY DO IT?

Termites nest belowground. So, why are their mounds so tall? It's all about staying comfortable. The mounds have tiny holes and a tall chimney. Scientists think that keeps termites cool during the day and warm at night. It also helps balance the flow of the gases oxygen and carbon dioxide to help them breathe.

BUSY BEAVERS CREATE PONDS

Beavers are born to build. By **instinct**, they know how to gnaw trees and use the branches to make dams. A dam blocks moving water from flowing any further. The water behind the dam spreads out. It reshapes dry land into a rich pond.

The ponds provide calm water for beavers to build their homes, called lodges. But they also affect the environment in many important ways. Ponds collect plentiful soil and nutrients for plants to grow. Then, worms and insects like dragonflies move in. Animals like birds and deer depend on these ponds for their food and habitat.

BY CHANGING THE FLOW OF WATER, BEAVER DAMS CAN ALSO HELP PROTECT THE ENVIRONMENT FROM FLOODS AND LONG PERIODS OF DRY WEATHER CALLED DROUGHTS.

NATURE'S CLEANUP CREW

Waste from **fertilizer** and other chemicals can pollute streams and creeks. This can harm drinking water and fish. Beavers play a part in keeping things clean! Beaver ponds provide a home for good bacteria and creatures like clams. They break down the bad chemicals to make the water clean.

HUNGRY BACTERIA EAT ROCKS

Tiny bacteria can reshape Earth too. The Rio Tinto is an unusual river in Spain. For thousands of years, people mined for gold, silver, and copper there. Its water is acidic, so fish can't survive. But some bacteria can! These bacteria get energy by "eating" rocks. This means that they oxidize (AWKS-uh-dize), or add oxygen to, the iron in them. This turns the river bright red!

These same bacteria also help form pyrite. Pyrite is a gold, sparkly mineral you can find in science stores and gem shops. The Rio Tinto has some of the largest pyrite supplies in the world.

The Rio Tinto is rich with iron and sulfur. So is the soil on Mars! Scientists think they can learn how microorganisms could live on Mars by studying the Rio Tinto.

PYRITE

DON'T BE FOOLED!

Pyrite gleams like gold—but it's not! During the Gold Rush, inexperienced diggers would sometimes find chunks of shiny pyrite. They thought they'd struck it rich. When they tried to cash it in, they found it wasn't worth much money at all. This earned pyrite the nickname "fool's gold."

UNDERWATER WORLDS

The lithosphere includes all parts of Earth's crust. Earth's crust extends below the oceans too. So, biogeology even happens underwater! In warm ocean waters, tiny animals called coral look for a place to live. Coral are related to jellyfish and come in many colors thanks to simple plantlike living things called algae.

Tiny polyps (PAHL-ups), or small tubelike coral, attach to rocks or other hard surfaces underwater. Then, something weird happens. As they grow, stony coral polyps secrete, or squeeze out, their own skeletons! Each skeleton is hard and cup-shaped. It's made of calcium carbonate, which is also known as limestone. These polyps build coral reefs.

CORAL SKELETONS ARE COMMONLY WHITE. BRIGHT COLORS SEEN IN REEFS OFTEN COME FROM ALGAE CORALS USE FOR FOOD.

CITIES OF THE SEA

Coral reefs only cover less than 2 percent of the ocean floor. However, scientists say 25 percent of all ocean creatures rely on them for food and habitat. Many sea creatures like fish, crabs, clams, oysters, and sea urchins live in them. Reefs also help nearby mangrove forests and seagrass beds stay healthy.

As stony coral grows and squeezes out its skeleton, the bones actually become part of the rock around it. Later, other coral polyps will attach on top of it. When many corals live together, their colony is called a coral reef.

Coral reefs can have hundreds of thousands of polyps. Only the top layer of a reef is alive. The big structure underneath is all rock and old skeletons. Today, coral reefs are in danger from **climate change**. Pollution and warming water can kill polyps and ruin the existing skeletons.

THE WORLD'S LARGEST REEF IS THE GREAT BARRIER REEF IN AUSTRALIA. IT'S MORE THAN 1,400 MILES (2,253 KM) LONG. YOU CAN SEE IT FROM OUTER SPACE!

AFTER

SLOW AND STEADY

Coral reefs can't grow back quickly if they're damaged. That's why it's important to protect them now. Each species is different, but some corals barely grow 1 inch (2.5 cm) in a year. The world's biggest reefs are between 5,000 and 10,000 years old!

HUMANS RESHAPE EARTH TOO

Humans reshape Earth in major ways. We build cities, roads, and power plants. We plow giant fields to grow food. How do humans create these things and keep them running? Often, we dig deep into Earth's crust for **resources** such as fossil fuels. These are matter, such as coal, natural gas, and oil, which formed over millions of years from plant and animal remains. Then, we burn them for energy.

Fossil fuel supplies may last for a while but not forever. The pollution from burning them harms the environment. It also leads to climate change. For our Earth to have a bright future, we need to think differently about how we use its resources.

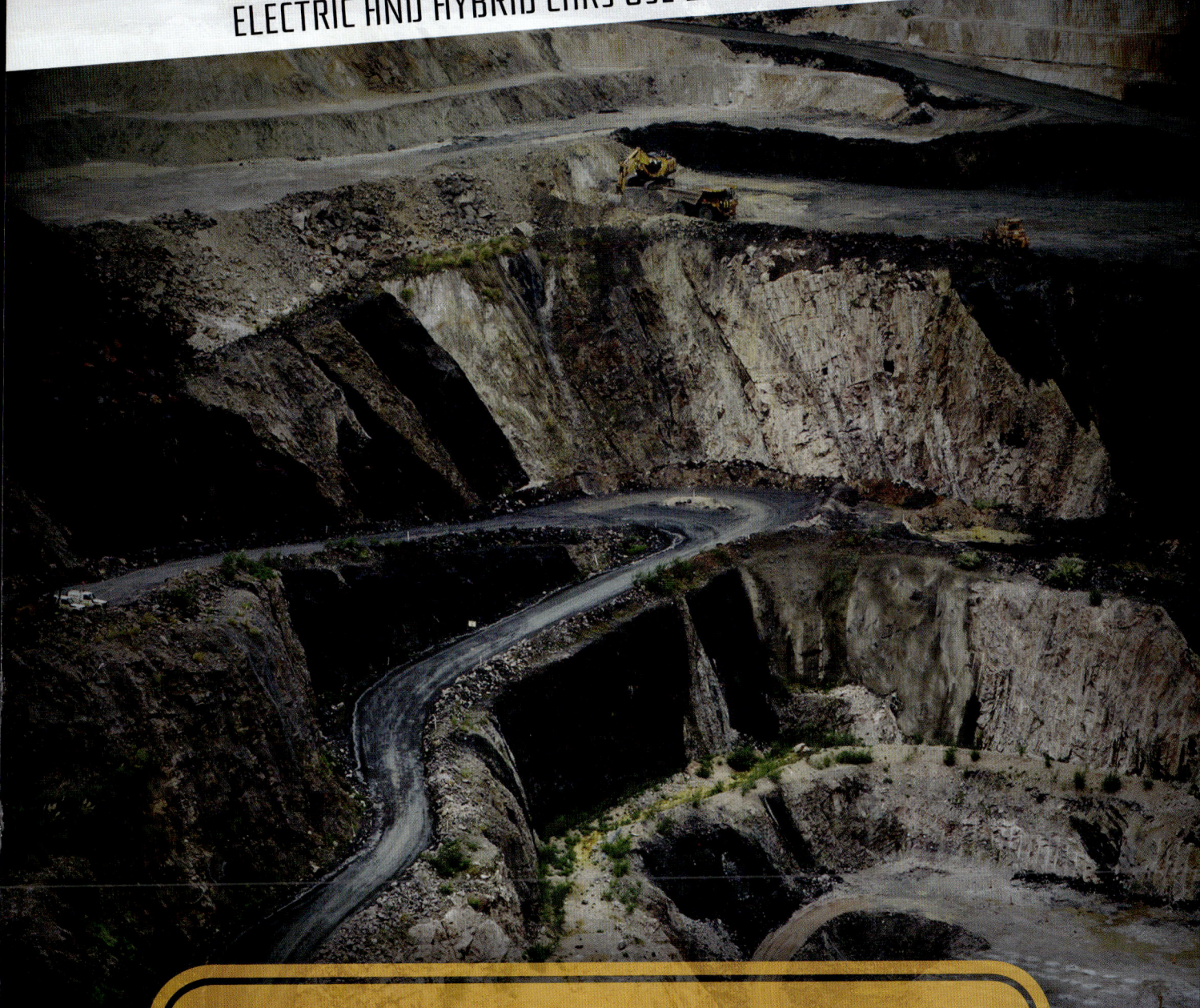

THIS IS A LITHIUM ORE MINE. LITHIUM IS USED TO MAKE BATTERIES THAT POWER OUR COMPUTERS AND SMARTPHONES. ELECTRIC AND HYBRID CARS USE LITHIUM BATTERIES TOO.

WHAT CAN YOU DO?

Two major causes of climate change are burning fossil fuels and **factory farms**. You can take small steps to help. Buy local products, and reuse what you have. Ask an adult to help you write a letter about your feelings on climate change. Then, send it to a local government official.

GLOSSARY

climate change: long-term change in Earth's climate, caused by human activities such as burning oil and natural gas

digestive system: the body parts having to do with eating, breaking down, and taking in food

environment: the conditions that surround a living thing and affect the way it lives

factory farm: a farm with a lot of livestock that is often raised indoors in conditions meant to increase profits while decreasing costs

fertilizer: something added to the soil that helps plants grow

fungus: a living thing that is somewhat like a plant, but doesn't make its own food, have leaves, or have a green color. Fungi include molds and mushrooms.

habitat: the place or type of place where a plant or animal naturally or normally lives or grows

instinct: an inborn reaction or behavior that aids in survival

mammal: a warm-blooded animal that has a backbone and hair, breathes air, and feeds milk to its young

nutrient: something a living thing needs to grow and stay alive

resource: a usable supply of something

suffix: a letter or a group of letters that is added to the end of a word to change its meaning or to form a new word

FOR MORE INFORMATION

BOOKS

Furstinger, Nancy. *Beaver Dams.* New York, NY: Weigl, 2019.

Kenney, Karen Latchana. *Termites.* Minneapolis, MN: Jump!, 2018.

Rake, Jody S. *Roots, Bulbs, and Bacteria: Growths of the Underground.* North Mankato, MN: Capstone Press, 2016.

WEBSITES

The Adventures of Herman
web.extension.illinois.edu/worms/
Find out Herman the Worm's favorite foods and see how his underground tunnels help the soil.

Prairie Dog
kids.nationalgeographic.com/animals/mammals/prairie-dog/
Learn cool facts and check out cute photos of these busy burrow builders.

What Is Climate Change?
www.wonderopolis.org/wonder/what-is-climate-change
Discover more important information about the causes of climate change and ways you can help.

Publisher's note to educators and parents: Our editors have carefully reviewed these websites to ensure that they are suitable for students. Many websites change frequently, however, and we cannot guarantee that a site's future contents will continue to meet our high standards of quality and educational value. Be advised that students should be closely supervised whenever they access the internet.

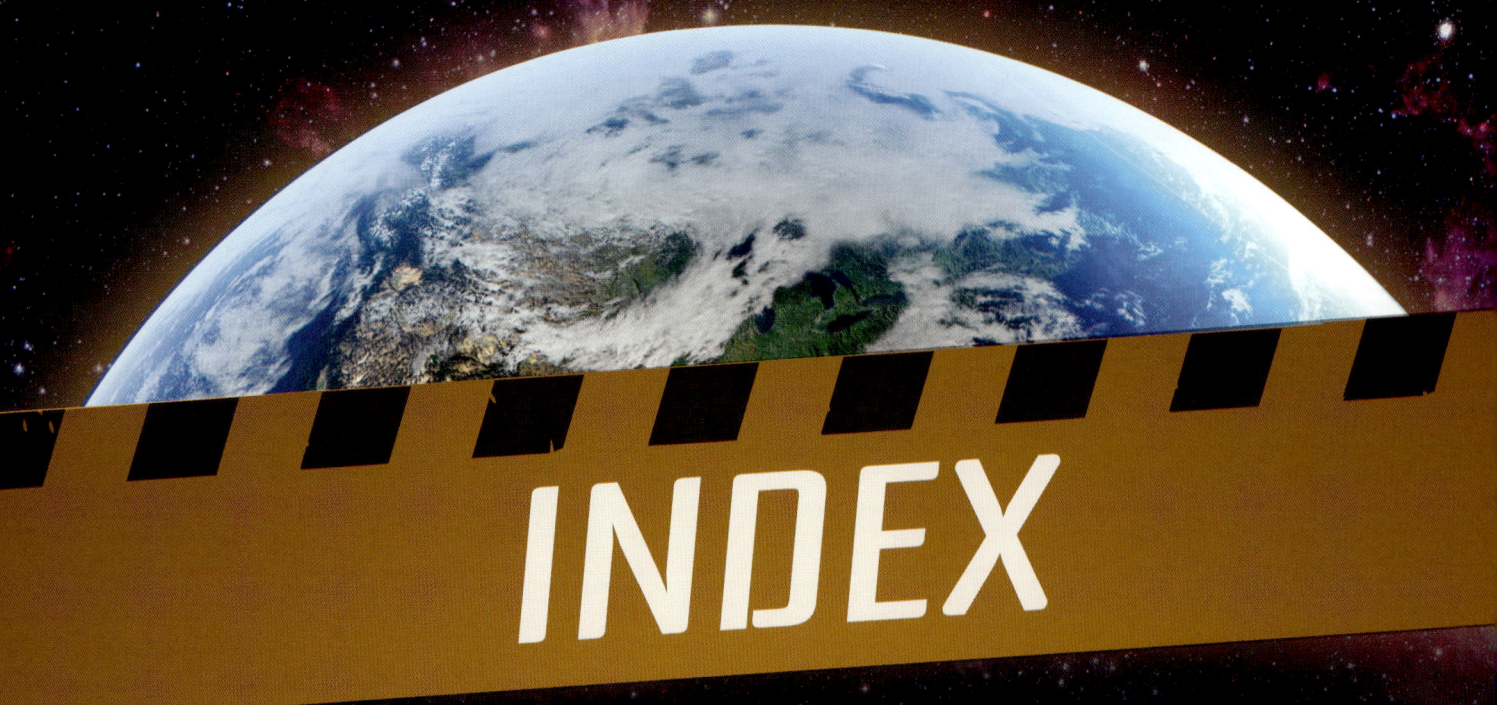

INDEX

animals 4, 6, 8, 9, 13, 14, 15, 16, 18, 20, 24, 28
bacteria 6, 9, 21, 22
beavers 4, 20, 21
biosphere 6, 7
burrow 14, 15, 16, 17
compost 11
coral 24, 25, 26, 27
crust 6, 24, 28
dam 4, 20, 21
erosion 10, 12, 13
farmers 12, 13
fossil fuels 28, 29
Great Barrier Reef 27
humans 7, 28
hydrosphere 6
kangaroo rat 14
lithosphere 6, 24
moles 14, 15
mound 15, 16, 18, 19
mudslide 13
ocean 6, 24, 25
plants 4, 6, 8, 10, 12, 13, 15, 20, 28
polyps 24, 26
prairie dog 16, 17
pyrite 22, 23
Rio Tinto 22, 23
roots 5, 7, 10, 12, 13, 15
soil 4, 5, 6, 8, 9, 10, 11, 12, 13, 15, 20, 23
termites 18, 19
worms 8, 10, 11, 15, 20